Chakras

7 Easy Guided Meditation Techniques For Awakening & Balancing Your Chakras: Meditation For Awakening Chakras

(How To Use The Law Of Attraction For Your Benefit)

Ezekiel Garrison

TABLE OF CONTENT

How Do I Know My Chakras Need Help? 1

Meditation's Role In Chakra Activation 12

Increasing Your Chakra System's Vitality 37

Crystals That Purify Each Chakra 43

Visualization And Sacral Meditation 69

Guided Imagery For Clearing Your Solar Plexus Chakra 87

A Third Eye That Is Open 100

Discover Your Love With The Heart Chakra 115

About Reflection 124

The Third Chakra, The Sacral Chakra 128

How Do I Know My Chakras Need Help?

Now that we have a greater understanding of the chakras, it is time to recognize when they begin to develop problems. Oftentimes, we are out of contact with our chakras, which can lead to numerous health and mental issues. However, because the majority of us do not realize that the chakras may be in need of assistance when coping with these issues, we frequently ignore them and do not give them the necessary attention.

Each chakra is significant and is responsible for a different part of the body, a different system, and even a distinct set of emotions. It is crucial to recognize when one of the chakras is not functioning as it should, and when something goes wrong, it is essential to know which chakra needs to be repaired. Here, we will examine each of the issues that can affect the chakras so that we can learn how to repair them and make them feel better!

difficulties with the root chakra

The root chakra will be affected whenever you feel unable to take care of your basic requirements or when you find it too difficult to organize your essentials. Whenever this begins to occur, you may sense that your prostates are affected, as well as issues with your immune system, male reproductive organs, legs, and feet. As a result of these problems, you may also experience degenerative arthritis, knee pain, sciatica, or dietary disorders.

As you can imagine, it is difficult when the root chakra is imbalanced, as it is unpleasant to experience so much discomfort in the legs and lower body. To restore equilibrium, you must begin to believe that you belong here and that you play a significant role. Once you have restored this equilibrium, you will once again feel connected, supported, and grounded in the world.

Having issues with the plexus chakra.

Whenever you have low self-esteem and are unable to believe in yourself, it is because the solar plexus chakra is underdeveloped. It will also suffer if you are concerned about criticism, particularly if you have received a great deal of criticism in the past or if you are self-conscious about your physical appearance. When the solar plexus chakra is out of balance, you may experience intestinal and colon problems, liver dysfunctions, elevated blood pressure, and even digestive issues.

When you want to restore the solar plexus chakra's optimal function, you must learn to embrace yourself regardless. You will not be perfect in your actions or your appearance, but you should embrace that these are a part of who you are. There are some things you are able to do and others you will never be able to do; accepting this will help you become more assertive and confident.

Disorders of the sacral chakra

This chakra will be affected if you are unable to effectively express your emotions and if you find it difficult to stick to your goals. It will be affected when you have an excessive amount of dread or when you give in to your addictions. It can also be impacted when you betray both yourself and the people around you. These issues will result in pelvic and back pain, reproductive organ issues, and urinary problems.

When you are ready to restore equilibrium, you must be creative, committed, and understand that it is acceptable to take risks. Additionally, you must learn to be sexual, outgoing, and impassioned. When you incorporate these into your daily existence, you will be able to respect yourself and others.

Issues relating to the heart chakra

When individuals are loved excessively or insufficiently, the heart chakra suffers. It will also suffer if you abandon others, if you become bitter or furious, or if you become envious. This will result in upper arm issues, shoulder issues, wrist discomfort, lymphatic system problems, asthma, and heart disease. Who would have thought that something as basic as one's affection for others could influence the number of health conditions one has?

There are some easy steps you can take to restore the equilibrium of your heart chakra. To achieve this, you must always make gratitude, compassion, and happiness your guiding principles. You must first learn how to extend forgiveness and then how to extend trust to others. When you are able to do so, when you have learned to value yourself and others, you will be more successful.

difficulties with the third vision

This is one of the most difficult chakras to work with, and it will not be simple to activate or work with. When you allow your emotions to begin to cloud your judgment, or when you become extremely irritable. It can also be impaired if your daydreams spiral out of control and your imagination takes over reality. When you do not contemplate on the current state of your life and become volatile, it is because the third eye requires assistance.

To alleviate some of this blockage, you must examine the larger picture of your life instead of spending so much time overanalyzing what is occurring. When you can see the bigger picture, you will have greater clarity and it will be simpler to focus on the things that require your attention rather than on those that are less significant. You can also use this method to identify your anxieties and stop them from controlling your life, and you will learn how to gain insight from others. When you clear away certain issues with the third eye, you will acquire greater wisdom and insight, and it will be easier to appreciate your life even more.

difficulty with the throat chakra

You will notice that the throat chakra is obstructed when you are unable to express your thoughts in writing or speech, or when you feel as though others are dictating your actions. This can frequently occur when you believe you have no say in the matter and that everyone else has the final say. This is the chakra you will need to focus on if you experience shoulder and neck pain, ear infections, ulcers, facial problems, thyroid issues, and irritated throats.

If you wish to restore equilibrium to this situation, you must learn how to be heard above the din. This implies that you must express your opinion and ensure that no one else determines your future. It is simpler to be a good listener, communicator, expressive, assertive, and honest when you know how to articulate your own opinions.

issues with the apex chakra

And finally, we must devote some attention to the crown chakra. When this one is blocked, it is usually because you are seeking a greater power than the one you already possess, and you will have difficulty figuring out how to use your skills and knowledge to their full potential. Occasionally, it will also be affected if you allow religious and political issues to bother you excessively, or if you overanalyze, bear prejudice, or fear being alone.

If you wish to prevent the crown chakra from becoming blocked, you must cultivate mental clarity and practice mindful living. When you are able to do this, it is simpler to live in the present and to have true and unshakeable wisdom and inner guidance. Obviously, this will take time to master and establish, but daily meditation and mindfulness practice can be extremely helpful.

Now that we have a better understanding of the factors that can obstruct each chakra, it is essential to learn the steps you can take to clear them. Numerous aspects of our daily lives can impact the chakras, and when they are neglected, it is more difficult to live the fulfilled and healthy life we desire. But once you identify the issues, it is much simpler to resolve them quickly.

Meditation's Role In Chakra Activation

Now that you are familiar with the locations and functions of your seven main chakras, you can move on to learning how to use meditation to activate your energy and aura and to open your chakras. Throughout meditation, you will utilize chakra mantras. Therefore, it is essential that we examine them initially.

Chakra Mantras

As stated previously, each of your chakras possesses a unique vibration. Sound is also a vibration. And there are songs with vibrational resonance with each of your chakras. These mantras, when used in meditation, can help to activate your chakras. The created vibrational resonance will eliminate the presence of energies that do not resonate with that chakra.

OM

This may be the most ubiquitous mantra in existence. OM is the primordial sound. It gathers your vitality in preparation for motion. This is also known as the acceptance mantra. This allows you to connect with your higher self and become more receptive to the energy flow within your body. It is the mantra for the seventh chakra, also known as the crown chakra. AH, the sound of release, is an alternative sound for the seventh charka, or you can choose to remain mute during meditation.

AUM (OM)

Utilize this mantra to purify and heal your Third Eye Chakra. This sound, when uttered during meditation, will liberate your inner wisdom from the constraints you have imposed on it.

HAM

Your spiritual voice is HAM. This mantra is used to clear the fifth chakra of impediments. Using this sound during meditation enables you to communicate your desires, requirements, and sense of self.

YAM

Utilize this mantra to purify the Heart chakra. This melody heals the heartache you are carrying and makes you more open to the possibility of loving once more.

RAM

This mantra is utilized to stimulate the third chakra. Using this sound while meditating will assist you in standing up for yourself. It improves your ability to stay true to your beliefs and control unwanted impulses. Utilize this mantra when you need to strengthen your self-control. Utilize it also when your self-esteem is low. This mantra should be chanted when experiencing anxiety.

VAM

The purpose of this mantra is to purify your sexual chakra. It is also beneficial for enhancing your self-image. When you have difficulty opening up in relationships, recite this mantra. Use it to increase your libido or if you have difficulty attaining sexual pleasure or orgasms.

LAM
This mantra is used to center oneself. Using this sound to cleanse your Root chakra releases blocked energies, allowing them to flow through your six other main chakras. Utilize this mantra when your vitality levels are low. Use this sound to reduce anxiety.

Meditation on the Chakra

I Am
This is a Root chakra meditation posture. The Tree Meditation Pose has an effect on your sense of survival. It aids in asserting your right to survive. It also affects the aspect of your existence that relates to your family relationships.

Spread your ankles apart in order to achieve balance.

Exhale. While doing so, allow your ankles to relax.

Allow your pelvic girdle to descend. Then, contract the quadriceps.

Raise your right foot and position it against the inner aspect of your left thigh. This manner, your weight is supported solely by your left foot. Rest the sole of your foot against your calf if you lack the flexibility or equilibrium to perform this.

Relax. Inhale. Allow gravity to ground you naturally. Imagine your body imbibing life-giving energy from the earth, as if you were a tree planted in the ground. Then, visualize the energy ascending your spine.

While performing this action, chant LAM and sense its effects on your Root chakra. Visualize the color red emanating from the energy center in your mind.

Hold this position as you inhale and exhale five times.

Then, change positions. Stand on your right foot and repeat the previous steps.

I Feel
This is a pose for sacral chakra meditation. The Goddess Meditation Pose is beneficial if you are experiencing fertility issues. In this context, fecundity refers not only to sexual activity and reproduction, but also to the capacity for creativity.

Stand with your feet extremely far apart. Make certain that your toenails are pointing outward.
Permit your pelvis to fall. Thus, your right knees and ankles will be in alignment.
Your palms should rest on your thighs.
Then, draw downward on your tailbone.
Repeatedly take several long breaths.
Next, make lateral movements with your limbs. Your pelvic region should sway back and forth. When you perform this movement, energy is drawn to your reproductive organs.

As you continue this movement for eight inhalations and exhalations, chant the mantra VAM.

Imagine a glowing orange light emanating from your second chakra.

I Do

This is the Solar Plexus chakra meditation pose. The Boat Meditation Pose has an effect on your productivity. It frees you from anxiety and prevents you from stagnating in life. This pose increases your confidence.

Begin by sitting with your legs extended out in front of you on the floor.

Then, bring your knees up to your torso.

Next, while supporting the back of your knees, lift your heels off the ground and maintain your balance. You are seated on the lower and back portion of your hipbone in this position.

While your shoulders are lowered, you should lift your torso and pull your stomach in. Send your weight forward and allow the front of your ischium to support it. This is also an excellent exercise for your abdominal muscles.

Forward extension of the upper extremities. Simultaneously, elevate your lower extremities.

Cross your arms across your torso as you exhale. Allow your lower extremities to descend gradually. Ensure that they are a few inches above the earth rather than completely touching it.

Reposition your body back into the boat position as you exhale.

Continue reiterating this at least five times. During this action, recite the mantra RAM. Similarly, visualize a yellow radiance emanating from your third chakra.

Following that, you may recline on your back.

I Love

This is your Heart chakra meditation posture. The Camel Meditation Pose affects your capacity for affection. Use this pose to promote the healing of past emotional wounds and the discharge of emotional hurts that have accumulated over the years. This pose should be practiced when you find it difficult to love or let go.

Assume a keeling position, ensuring there is adequate space between your knees. Create a space that is as wide as your pelvis.

Then, recline so that your weight is supported by your ankles.

The hands should lie on the chest, and the toes should be curled.

Elevate yourself. In this position, the pelvis are above the knees.

Then, position your palms on your lower back, fingers pointing upward. Simultaneously, pull your sacrum downwards as you raise your anterior hipbones upwards.

Then, lean backwards and tilt your head until it is extremely extended. Use your palms to support your heels. Before you arch your back, visualize someone or something that you adore. Offer this action to that individual or target.

Maintain the position. Slow your respiration down. Imagine a green radiance emanating from your heart as you chant YAM.

Repeatedly take deep breaths and then realign the cranium and sacrum.

Recline on your heels. Then, place your hand back on your bosom. Lastly, lower your head with reverence.

I Speak

This posture is a meditation for the Throat chakra. This meditation posture, also known as the Supported Shoulder Stand, focuses on truth, expression, and the etheric.

Start by reclining down on a yoga mat. Utilize creased fabrics to provide shoulder support. Nevertheless, rest your head on the earth.

Fold your knees and position your legs over your head by moving your hips upwards. Utilize your forearms to support your middle back.

Raise one leg while ensuring the heels point upward. Keep your forearms supporting your middle back. Then, lift the opposite limb.

Concentrate on your inhalations and exhalations simultaneously. Observe the movement of your chest as it rises and descends.

Hold this position for several minutes while reciting the HAM mantra. Imagine a brilliant blue light flooding your throat chakra.

When finished, slowly lower one leg followed by the other.

I See

The Third Eye chakra meditation posture. True to its moniker, the Easy Meditation Pose is a position that anyone, regardless of flexibility, can perform. This meditation pose stimulates the extrasensory senses. Moreover, it influences the functions of each of the seven chakras.

While seated on the floor, tuck your ankles toward your groin.

Connect the tips of your right hand's digits to those of your left. It is known as the Hakini Mudra.

With eyes closed, take ten deep breaths in and out.

Concentrate on the inhaling and exhaling sounds.

Move your tongue so that its tip contacts your palate with each inhalation. Then separate it with each exhale.

Next, rest your forearms on your knees for at least five minutes. Simultaneously, chant the OM mantra. Imagine your Third Eye chakra emitting a violet radiance.

I Understand

This is the Crown chakra meditation pose. The Corpse Meditation Pose facilitates entry into the spiritual domain.

Recline on your back. Ensure that your comfort is met. This includes placing a pillow under your head, a blanket over your body, or towels under your knees, as well as ensuring that the room temperature is neither too hot nor too chilly. You may hold this position for quite some time.

Your legs should be separated by a distance equal to the width of your pelvis.

Permit your arms to hang loosely at your sides. However, your forearms should be facing upward.

Deepen your respiration.

Then, while tensing your entire body, raise your head, arms, and legs from the floor.

Maintain this position while reciting the OM mantra. Visualize a brilliant white light emanating from your Crown chakra.

When it is time to discharge, exhale through the mouth.

Repeat this process several times.

Imagine a lotus flower perched atop your cranium in your imagination. As you inhale, visualize it opening and blossoming. As the blossom opens, divine light flows into it.

Imagine that you are expelling all the negative, toxic, and unproductive energies from your body as a black vapor as you exhale.

Continue this mental exercise for five minutes.

When you are prepared to leave your meditative state, gradually restore your awareness by focusing on the movement of your respiration. Consider moving your fingertips and toes. Gradually perceiving the movement will enable you to reconnect with your physical body.

The various chakras in your body require periodic cleansing, and we have already discussed some of the meditational practices that you can employ. In this section, we will examine additional meditational poses you can attempt.

Om meditation

"om" meditation is the first form of meditation. This is a very straightforward method for purifying your chakras. It rose to prominence in the 1970s and remains one of the most popular forms of meditation. It is quite easy and requires little effort.

To execute: To execute this technique, lie on the floor with your legs folded. Keep your back erect and rest the backs of your hands on your knees. This position is more commonly known as the lotus pose. Take several long breaths and gradually close your eyes. Chant one of the words such as "om" or "lam" You must recite for 15 minutes non-stop. Avoid becoming distracted by external factors. Choose a gloomy room and ensure that all windows are open to allow for the circulation of fresh air. You can perform this twice daily for 15 minutes.

Kundalini meditation

As you are aware, the chakras in your body rotate to maintain your health. In the end, however, they are affected and cease functioning or operate intermittently. This can be resolved through kundalini meditation. This meditation is simple to perform, and you can begin whenever you wish.

To execute: To execute this meditation, begin by sitting in the lotus position. Take several long breaths and then close your eyes. Imagine a tiny orb of light emanating from your root chakra. The orb collects all of the negative energy from the chakra before moving to the chakra located above it. Before proceeding to the third chakra, it pulls all negativity from the sacral chakra. In a similar fashion, it advances to the fourth, then the fifth, the sixth, and ultimately the seventh. All negativity is expelled, and your chakras resume their proper rotation. After collecting all of the negative energy from your chakras, the light ball exits your body by penetrating your cranium and leaving your body. Once more, a new ball arises from your primary chakra. Continue to visualize this for fifteen minutes.

Qi gong meditation

Qi gong is the answer for those who are not interested in the previous type of meditation and are searching for something simpler. Qi gong is simple to execute and yields the same benefits as the previous form of meditation.

To execute: To execute this meditation, sit in a quiet room and adopt the lotus position. Then, take several long breaths and close your eyes. Imagine now a small airball emanating from your first chakra. It then proceeds to the heart chakra after cleansing this chakra. During this process, it purifies all organs in its path. The energy then travels to the final chakra before returning to the heart chakra. The blood then descends to your first and then returns to your heart. So, instead of exiting your body, it continues to move alongside it. You can complete this daily in 15 minutes. You can also visualize an orb of light, similar to the previous method.

Walking contemplation

It is a common misconception that meditation consists solely of sitting still and repeating a word. The practice of meditating while strolling is known as "walking meditation" Walking meditation is a form of meditation in which the practitioner walks while contemplating.

To perform: To perform this type of meditation, seek out an open field. You must have sufficient space to proceed in a straight line and then circle back to the starting point. Begin by standing tall with your hands at your sides. Now begin walking in a straight line while observing your feet. When you place your left foot in front, take a deep inhalation, and when you place your right foot in front, exhale. You must maintain this, and you can use a signal, such as a gong, that instructs you to place your legs forward. Once you reach the opposite side, you should turn around and walk to the opposite side. If you don't have a long aisle to walk down, you can also walk in a circle, but be careful not to become disoriented.

Zazen meditation

Zazen meditation is another form of movement-based meditation similar to walking meditation. In addition to being simple to perform, zazen requires no movement.

To perform: To perform this type of meditation, select a peaceful area of your home. Kneel on the ground and cross your legs beneath your body. You can rest your feet flat or prop them up by using your toes as support. Start swaying your body forward and backward immediately. Try to maintain as much balance as possible and avoid collapsing repeatedly. You must maintain a consistent motion and have fun while rocking your body. Do this daily for 15 minutes.

Meditation with a heartbeat

Heart beat meditation is a form of meditation that focuses the mind and body on the heart. Due to its simplicity, it is one of the most widely practiced disciplines worldwide.

To perform this type of meditation, you must assume a comfortable seated position. It need not be on the floor, and the lotus position is optional. Seat yourself on a chair or the bed. Now, take several long breaths. Place your right hand over your heart and listen to its rhythm. Now envision your heart pumping clean, oxygenated blood to the rest of your body as it continues to beat. It is entirely nourishing your body, and all of your cells are functioning optimally. Your chakras are revolving appropriately, and you feel vibrant. Do this daily for 15 minutes.

Meditation on respiration

Breathing meditation is more commonly referred to as yoga-based meditation. It is simple to execute and will leave you feeling thoroughly energized.

Pranayama

Begin by resting in the lotus position and taking deep breaths. Now, close your right nostril with your right forefinger and inhale through your left. Then, close the left nostril and exhale through the right. Re-inhale through your right nostril, then close it and exhale through your left. Maintain this for 10 minutes.

Kapalbhati

To perform: To perform this, take a long breath in and then concentrate on your exhaled breath. You must exhale more than you inhale.

Bhrastrika

To conduct this type of meditation, assume the lotus position while seated. Next, stoop while taking a deep inhalation, then raise your head while exhaling.

Guided visualization meditation

Guided visualization is an effective form of meditation that will purify your chakras immediately. It is one of the most frequently prescribed forms of meditation for individuals rehabilitating from illness.

Start by taking a long breath in order to perform this type of meditation. You may recline on your sofa or cot if you so choose. Now, picture yourself lying on a field of lush verdant grass. You are beaming as you gaze upon the brilliant sun. All of your problems have vanished, and your body is in perfect condition. You feel like a brand-new person and adore your existence. You can also visualize swimming in a river or resting in a forest. Anything that aids in mental retreat is acceptable. Do this for twenty minutes per day and you will see how your life has improved!

Hypnotic concentration

In hypnosis meditation, you induce a trance and journey into your subconscious. It is somewhat complex, and you may need to practice it a few times to perfect it.

To conduct this type of meditation, one must recline on a couch. Make sure you don't lie down in a dark room as you might fall unconscious. Attempt to stay as alert as feasible. Now close your eyes and venture to the depths of your mind. Examine the area in question to determine if something is troubling you. If something is, make an effort to comprehend it correctly. Perhaps you can remedy the situation and find a solution. Once you are finished, carefully rise and record what you observed.

Mindfulness practice

This is the most basic type of meditation. It is one of the most straightforward and effective modes of meditation.

To execute: To execute this technique, rest in the lotus position and take deep breaths. Place a plant or something similar to a Buddha statue in front of you. Now, gaze at the statue with your eyes partially closed. Smile softly as you continue to gaze at it. Concentrate on the object alone and ignore everything else. Ensure that you are surrounded by no distractions.

It is advisable to progressively increase the time. After about a week, you can increase it to 17 minutes, then 20 minutes, and so on. Daily meditation should last at least 30 minutes.

When you desire to mediate, you must take care of a number of essentials. This includes utilizing the proper illumination, having fresh air flow into the room, having an inspirational object such as a Buddha statue in the room, etc. Another thing to observe is that singing bowls can be utilized. You are provided with a mallet with which to strike the circumference of a metal singing bowl. It produces a calming and tranquil sound that aids concentration during practice.

If you experience any discomfort, you should cease immediately and not continue. If dizziness occurs, remain still for five minutes and then steadily rise from your current position.

Increasing Your Chakra System's Vitality

The remainder of this book will focus on specific areas of alternative therapy and how they can assist you in balancing your heart chakra. But you can also regain balance by making modifications to your general way of life.

Our modern way of life can wreak havoc on the heart chakra. We spend so much time indoors, shut off from the natural world, that sometimes we don't even breathe natural fresh air for days, moving from the home, to the car, to the office, or some other 'inside' location to spend the working hours.

We have lost our connection with the natural world, often being unaware of the phase of the moon at night or the origin of our food outside of the supermarket. The majority of us have lost touch with natural food, purchasing and consuming processed, pre-packaged, and takeout dishes that often do not even resemble food.

Even information and entertainment can be detrimental to our energy field.

The television, movies, and social media are replete with negative messages, including violence, rage, wars, misery, peril, selfishness, out-of-control self-interest, and human catastrophe. All of them exemplify extremely negative energy, which is their only shared characteristic.

These are the types of issues that can obstruct the heart chakra and lead to difficulties in life; however, how can you alter this?

Taking the time to'smell the flowers' can have a profound effect on your energy field.

Spend time outdoors, breathing fresh air and walking on the earth rather than concrete. Spend no time jogging, cycling, or participating in active sports. All of that may be beneficial to your physical health, but you also need slow time, time spent strolling in a garden or park, time spent wandering in the countryside or along the coast, and time spent admiring the work you've done in your garden.

Taking the time to breathe real, pure air and making time for yourself in your life is not at all selfish. We have been conditioned to believe that taking time for oneself is the worst form of selfishness, particularly but not exclusively for women. We are accustomed to putting everyone and everything ahead of our own requirements, but taking time for yourself is the antithesis of selfishness.

When you allow yourself time to heal, balance your energy field, and relax, you will be better able to interact with others and accomplish more in less time and with less effort.

We are a part of nature, and being in nature nourishes our energy field, so try going for a walk in a park or in the countryside, where you can smell the fragrance of nature, observe the color of the flowers, and feel the texture of the trees. A stroll on the beach can fill your lungs with fresh air, and walking barefoot on the sand is both a unique experience and a good exfoliator for your feet.

Being conscious of the seasons, the phases of the moon, and the ancient festivals of nature is a marvelous way to reconnect with the earth's natural energy and our own natural energy.

If you have access to a garden or outdoor space, you should utilize it. Growing flowers can add elegance to your life, while growing your own herbs and vegetables can not only provide you with fresh air and exercise, but also provide you with fresh, organic ingredients for cooking. There is nothing more delicious than a freshly harvested salad from your garden, balcony, or windowbox.

You should also work to develop and strengthen your relationships with others. Our personal lives can become extremely limited and lonely. Numerous individuals reside alone or in a series of brief relationships. Even when we are part of a positive relationship or a loving family, it is not uncommon for us to not even know our next-door neighbors, to live in an area with no ties to the surrounding community, and to treat our residence as a dormitory rather than a home. This sensation of social isolation can damage the energy of the heart chakra and deplete your vital energy over time.

Make an effort to communicate with others. Join organizations, socialize locally, become involved in your local church, or join a club.

A healthy energy field and chakra system requires a sense of belonging and sharing, as well as a connection to and willingness to aid others.

Crystals That Purify Each Chakra

The Mineral Kingdom is a repository of restorative light accessible to all. In the same manner that some crystals work with a single chakra, many work with multiple chakras, and a select few work with all of them.

They can be used in place of or in addition to a traditional Chakra Crystal Set.

Wearing or carrying these potent crystals can help maintain clear, balanced, or aligned chakras. They range from readily available crystals, such as Quartz, that should be included in every crystal collection to uncommon and unusual stones for you to discover.

First, we will examine the crystals that purify your seven chakras. Then, we will examine the various techniques and methods you can use to utilize the energies of these crystals for clearing your chakras of negative or blocked energy.

Crystals that purify each Chakra:

Quartz Crystal

Useful Forms: Pebble, Crystal Point, and Crystal Wand

Quartz is the most prevalent mineral on Earth. It ranges in color from transparent to white, but the clear varieties have the greatest cleansing properties.

White light purifies the chakras as a result of the cleansing properties of Clear Quartz. It anchors and transmits energies of high vibration in a very direct and precise manner. Additionally, this crystal absorbs negative energies, preventing them from inflicting harm.

Angel Aura Forms Utilizable: Tumble Stone, Crystal Point

Additionally referred to as Opal Aura. This is a Quartz crystal bonded with precious metals such as Silver and Titanium. This results in a transparent crystal with pastel spectrum hues.

With its celestial energy and high vibration, this cleansing crystal purifies all seven chakras. With its rainbow radiance, it expels lower energies and also balances the chakras.

Libyan Desert Glass Forms usable: unpolished crystal Also known as Libyan Gold Tektite. These stones were formed when an ancient meteor impacted the dunes of the Sahara Desert. This clouded golden crystal has a matte surface and a crater-like or rippled exterior.

Creates an influx of purifying, golden light that purifies all chakras. Extremely effective on severely clogged chakras or persistent energy obstructions.

Tibetan Black Quartz Forms of Use: Also referred to as Tibetan Quartz and Tibetan Black Spot Quartz. In the Himalayas, these crystals primarily develop as double-terminated Crystal Points. They are a smoky color, and many of them contain black carbon inclusions or phantom formations.

Tibetan Black Quartz has cleansing properties because it absorbs negative energies from the chakras and aura like a sponge. These crystals transform these energies, but they must be periodically cleansed because they can become overwhelmed.

Selenite Forms Utilizable: Tumble Stone, Unpolished Crystal, Crystal Wand Description: A delicate white crystal named after the Greek moon goddess Selene. Its crystal structure reflects light and causes it to glimmer like moonlight.

Perhaps not surprisingly, this crystal has access to the purifying properties of the Moon. Selenite emits a purifying shower of celestial light throughout the chakras. It effortlessly removes negative or obstructed energies.

Serpentine Usable Forms: Tumble Stone, Crystal Wand Description: Serpentine is available in a variety of green to yellow-green hues. The stone may be opaque or translucent. Some varieties have a pattern reminiscent of snakeskin, hence the name.

Serpentine is an expert at purifying all chakras and the luminous pathway that connects them. Its spiraling green light purifies dense, detrimental energies and makes room for the entry of new light.

Moldavite Usable Forms: Unadorned Crystal

Description: These uncommon forms of Tektite were created by a massive meteor impact in what is now the Czech Republic millions of years ago. These glassy stones have a wavy surface and are an earthy dark green hue.

This crystal's cleansing properties are not for the timid of heart. Moldavite is one of the planet's most potent purifying crystals. It swiftly purges the entire Chakra System with its emerald-green fire and is a potent cleanser and detoxifier of trapped or negative energies.

Methods for Using a Single Crystal to Purify Your Chakras

The most effective way to utilize these profoundly purifying crystals is to position them directly into the chakras or to meditate with them. The majority of these crystals are available as Tumble Stones or as refined crystals, but there are a few other options to consider.

First, we will examine a technique with which you are more familiar, which employs a Tumble Stone or polished crystal. If you do not wish to incorporate the Soul Star or Earth Star Chakras into any of these techniques, you can simply move on to the next chakra.

How to Cleanse Your Chakras (Lying Down) with a Single Tumble Stone

As you would when selecting crystals for a Chakra Crystal Set, ensure that your crystal has at least one flat surface so that it can be securely placed on the body. If the crystal you possess is not a Tumble Stone, use a polished or unpolished crystal instead.

Find a peaceful and comfortable spot to sleep.

Place your crystal approximately 6 inches beneath your feet, within the Earth Star Chakra.

Lie face-up on the ground and assume a comfortable position. Take several in-depth breaths. Close your eyes and visualize yourself as being a large strong tree with roots going deep into the Earth.

See your roots reaching the very center of the Earth where they wrap around a large Iron crystal.

Sit up and move the crystal to your Root Chaka location. Lay back and relax for about a minute or longer if you prefer.

Then move the crystal up to the Sacral Chakra. Continue up the chakras leaving the crystal on each chakra for about a minute.

Place the crystal approximately 6 inches above the crown of your cranium for the Soul Star Chakra.

Before rising again, please open your eyes and take a few moments to reflect.

How to Cleanse Your Chakras (Sitting) with a Single Tumble Stone

Similar to the previous procedure, but this one requires the use of your arms. This will become simpler with practice, much like a yoga pose.

Cross your legs or sit in a chair and take several long breaths.

Place the crystal on the floor between your legs or beneath the chair. This corresponds to the Earth Star Chakra.

Visualize yourself as a large, sturdy tree with profound roots in the ground.

Imagine your roots reaching the center of the planet, where they encircle a massive iron crystal.

Next, place your crystal in the position of your Root Chakra using both palms. Close your eyes and maintain this position for approximately one minute, or longer if desired.

Continue to ascend the crystal through each chakra. Spending roughly a minute with each individual.

The Soul Star Chakra must be held with both palms approximately 6 inches above the head. The shape of your limbs should be circular.

Once completed, carefully set the crystal down. Raise and shake out your limbs.

Before rising again, please open your eyes and take a few moments to reflect.

Utilization of Crystal Points and Wands

Some crystals, such as a Crystal Point, can be found in their natural crystal form. Typically, they have six sides and a point on one or both extremities. Crystal Wands are typically cut and polished crystals with facets comparable to a natural Crystal Point. Some wands have no facets and are seamless. They are referred to as Crystal Massage Wands.

Tumble Stones emit energies in all directions, whereas Crystal Points and cut Tumble Stones do not. Crystal Wands direct and concentrate energy at their tips. Due to the fact that their energies can be directed towards the chakras without location, for instance, crystals are very popular among crystal healers.

Using a Crystal Point or Wand to Purify Your Chakras

Using a Crystal Point or Crystal Wand to work on oneself is more involved than using a Chakra Crystal Set. You may, of course, have a friend who shares your beliefs use the crystal on your chakras.

While seated with crossed legs or on a chair, grasp your crystal in your dominant hand.

Close your eyes and inhale several inhalations.

Visualize yourself as a large, sturdy tree with profound roots in the ground.

Imagine your roots reaching the center of the planet, where they encircle a massive iron crystal.

Open your eyes, lower your hand, and point your crystal at the Earth Star Chakra, which is located somewhere beneath your feet.

Direct your crystal towards this chakra in a small clockwise circular motion for approximately one minute, or longer if you desire.

Proceed to the Root Chakra next. You can now direct the crystal inwards towards this area and use circular motions for approximately one minute.

Clear each of the Major Chakras as you ascend the hierarchy. For the Crown Chakra, direct the crystal downwards toward the crown of your cranium.

As before, direct the crystal in a circular motion upwards, just above the crown of your head, for the Soul Star Chakra. Take a moment before getting back up.

How to Cleanse Your Chakras Through Meditation Using a Single Crystal

Meditations and visualizations are becoming increasingly popular as a means of chakra cleansing and balancing. You can use any type of crystal for chakra cleansing. With a natural Crystal Point or Crystal Wand in your palms, the crystal should be pointing upwards.

Close your eyes and cross your legs or sit on a chair with your legs crossed.

Hold the crystal in your lap while taking several deep breaths.

Visualize yourself as a large, sturdy tree with profound roots in the ground.

Imagine your roots reaching the center of the planet, where they encircle a massive iron crystal.

Visualize the crystal you are holding glowing with light as you concentrate on it.

Visualize a white laser beam penetrating your Soul Star Chakra. Observe this chakra shining like a white star for one minute.

Imagine this beam of light moving into your Crown Chakra, which also radiates brightly like a star. Repeat this procedure throughout each chakra.

Spending roughly a minute with each individual.
Before rising again, please open your eyes and take a few moments to reflect.

The Spiritual Body

Chakras are openings through which energy enters and exits the aura, which is our energy body. We are like organisms in the surrounding energy sea. Each of these vortices is engaged in a continuous energy exchange with the Universal Energy Field. The chakras are genuinely open when we speak of feeling "open"
Maintaining open Chakras is a lifelong endeavor. The mission of the spiritual seeker is to remain receptive to the energies of the cosmos regardless of what occurs.
On a conscious level, we typically experience these energy exchanges through our five senses: sight, sound, scent, and touch. However, we also receive energy in other ways. When we experience a flash of intuition,

illumination, inspiration, or profound inner knowing, it is because our astral bodies have allowed energy from realms beyond the ordinary sensory realm to enter, and we perceive this energy exchange as information ascending to the level of consciousness.

It is essential to open the Chakras and increase our energy flow because the more freely we allow energy to circulate, the healthier we are. Physical illness is induced by an energy imbalance or a blockage in the flow of energy. A lack of flow in the human energy system causes disease, distorts our perceptions and dampens our emotions, and impedes our ability to experience pleasure and the fullness of life.

In addition to being energy portals, your Chakras store the karmic lessons of present and prior lives. You may have chosen certain Chakra limitations for this particular lifetime because your essence desired to learn specific lessons. Before incarnation, we sometimes place obstacles and limitations on our paths in order to coerce ourselves into awakenings we would not have otherwise pursued.

The development of the Chakras is significantly influenced by our formative experiences. When we are discouraged, shamed, or punished for certain behaviors, our typical response is to withdraw and block the sensation, thereby preventing energy flow through the corresponding Chakra. We may abandon certain behaviors out of dread or shame, which can result in energy body atrophy or entropy.

Long-term, this pattern results in the deterioration or disfigurement of the corresponding Chakra. Some of us have Chakras that rotate in the opposite direction, or anti-clockwise. Others' Chakras are extremely contracted and stagnant. In the case of extremely severe disease, which always originates at the level of the energy body, a Chakra can actually rupture.

However, regardless of what life tosses at you, you always have the ability to heal yourself.

It is also essential to realize that if you have developed a blockage in a particular Chakra, this is the result of a compassionate act of self-preservation initiated by your subconscious mind. Your subconscious was attempting to shield you from harm and suffering, and as a result, it shut down an entire faculty to prevent you from facing a disagreeable reality. This occurs frequently during childhood, when the conscious mind is insufficiently developed to comprehend and assimilate the experience in a proportional and balanced manner.

Therefore, if you have a blockage in your energy body, you should not feel guilty, ashamed, or enraged. It is the result of a well-intentioned impulse of self-preservation, and it indicates that in an earlier stage of your development, an unconscious mechanism activated in an effort to keep you secure.

To heal this condition, you must restore energy passage through the affected Chakra. When the energy flow through a

Chakra is increased, psychological information is conveyed to consciousness. This can include the surfacing of repressed memories, revelations, heightened dream activity, the release of repressed grief or wrath, and even physical detox or cleansing symptoms.

A new season of the planetary cycle commences every 52 days. One of the seven visible planets "rules" the Earth for 52 days, during which its archetypal energy is amplified on the planet. For each planetary season, the Chakra associated with the governing planet is more receptive to its influence.

The cycle of planetary seasons enables us to concentrate on one Chakra at a time. This is a highly advantageous method of working with energy fields, as we can carefully open each Chakra and process the released personal material one Chakra at a time.

Having a Chakra system that is completely open enables us to absorb a great deal of energy from the Universal field. Being truly "open" entails allowing a great deal of vibrational input on the level of the etheric body and assimilating and integrating a great deal of empirical data on the level of the conscious mind, particularly during dramatic moments in our lives.

This is a difficult undertaking, and the majority of us cannot complete it all at once. Simply, there would be excessive input. A sudden flow of energy through all of the Chakras would discharge too much psychological material, and we would be unable to process all of the new information.

When we align this inner work with the "cosmic schedule" of planetary cycles, we venerate each Chakra and planetary energy without rushing awakening or transformation. Allowing the implanted germ of each archetypal energy to fully blossom within us, in its own time, brings us into balance.

This process reorients and reconfigures the structure of your entire being, restoring cosmic equilibrium to your core. You will learn how to align your energy with the principles that govern the cosmos, thereby profoundly enhancing the powers of your body, heart, mind, and spirit. You will be able to completely integrate yourself into the Cosmos while simultaneously incorporating the energies of the Cosmos into yourself.

You can access the ethereal realms of cosmic energy and draw health, prosperity, and good fortune from the forces of All-That-Is with this cosmic understanding of the structure of your astral or light body.

When you operate in accordance with the universe's fundamental structure, the universe's mighty forces accompany your every thought, word, and deed!

You Consist of Light

This book will teach you how to draw into the forces of the universe, the forces that create worlds. These capabilities are present within you at this very moment. In fact, you were born with these abilities, and it is your birthright to utilize them.

There is an abundance of gifts, knowledge, wisdom, and authority within you. You possess extraordinary, extraterrestrial powers to transform your life and manifest pleasure and well-being.

The universe is electrical in nature. Our bodies are electrical conduits. Everything in our world, including the food we consume, the water we drink, the air we breathe, the clothes we wear, and the roofs over our heads, is composed of energy. This is what mystery traditions refer to as "akasha" or primordial radiance.

Our senses inform us that we are surrounded by numerous distinct objects. According to occult teachings, however, there is only one entity of which we are all a part. Modern science confirms this, and physicists now envision the universe as a vast ocean of pulsating electromagnetic energy.

Because our physical senses are what they are, this electro-magnetic "one thing" appears to the human mind to be composed of separate entities.

For instance, the chair you are seated on is composed of atoms, which, when viewed through a microscope, are predominantly vacant space. On a molecular scale, the distance between a nucleus and an electron is proportional to the thousands of light-years between the Sun and an orbiting planet. Regardless of how it may appear to your limited sensibilities, you are in fact sitting on a vast expanse of nothingness.

The chair also appears motionless, but it is actually a rhythmic pulsation of spinning forces and an electron dance. It only appears to be a chair in your mind because your sensory apparatus is tuned to specific vibrational frequencies.

Humans have been conditioned to consider as "real" only what they can perceive with their sensory faculties, but this is analogous to blindfolding oneself and claiming that only darkness is real!

If the range of your senses were slightly expanded, you would be able to perceive a vastly different world, containing entities that you cannot even conceive of right now (even though they exist!).

Consider the fact that certain species of fish have only two-dimensional vision. Their perceptual range precludes the majority of what we can see. From the perspective of a fish, "reality" is a mere fraction of what we consider reality to be. There are animals that can perceive aspects of reality that humans cannot. For instance, cats can see infrared frequencies that the human eye cannot; their reality includes objects that are in no way "real" to us. The human body/mind interface experiences a minuscule frequency range known as visible light, and there is a vast majority of the universe that falls outside of this frequency range. Dogs can perceive sound frequencies that are far too high for the human ear to detect. However, if you have ever blown a dog whistle and observed its effect on your dog, you cannot deny that the sound is genuine, even if you cannot hear it.

All of this demonstrates that the five human senses of sight, sound, taste, touch, and smell only provide a limited glimpse into reality.

You have been instructed to identify yourself with your physical physique. You have been taught to believe that you are Emily Smith, born in 1985 in Boston, MA, that you are an American, a Democrat, and that you weigh 130 lbs., and that this information is fundamental to your identity.

In reality, you are much, much more than the physical vehicle of your body and its worldly experiences, imprisoned in the linear timeline of this incarnation. Your essential, fundamental nature is consciousness. Not structure. Not your physical organism. "We are not merely humans having a spiritual experience." We are spiritual creatures experiencing human life." – Pierre Teilhard de Chardin

You are an infinite, eternal consciousness experiencing a particular human experience. You constantly partake in the abundance of the Universal Energy Field, and the entirety of the cosmos resides within you. You alone are responsible. You are it. You are composed of the Cosmic Light. You are One with It at this very moment.

You have access to levels of consciousness that far transcend your ordinary mental capabilities. The entire cosmic library of information is available for distribution. You have access to immense powers that can help you create the life of your desires. They are already within you because your electromagnetic fields are identical.

Changing your sense of self-identity is necessary if you wish to utilize your inherent abilities. You must relinquish the notion that you are a finite and limited being and step into the truth of who you are, which is infinite and limitless.

Visualization And Sacral Meditation

Meditation is a method for calming the mind, becoming conscious of one's thoughts and emotions, and achieving inner serenity. Meditation has been shown to have numerous health benefits, including reduced tension and anxiety, enhanced concentration, improved sleep, and enhanced immunity. Meditation can be practiced anywhere, at any time, and can be enjoyed by anyone.

There are numerous methods of meditation. You can practice mindfulness meditation by concentrating on your breath, repeating a mantra, or engaging in seated or walking meditation. In addition, you can use a variety of objects as meditation aids, including music, candlelight, and art. All of these aid in opening the lower chakras and integrating the energies of Svadhisthana into daily life.

This chapter on sacral meditation and visualization delves deeper into the various techniques used to open this chakra and provides useful starting points. So, let's plunge in.

Visualization and Meditation

Meditation and visualization are two of the most prevalent methods for opening the sacral chakra. Meditation is an ancient practice that dates back thousands of years. Meditation is an exercise that allows you to concentrate on one object or thought while erasing all other thoughts. Mantras, which are sacrosanct sounds spoken or chanted during meditation, are frequently employed. Mantras are utilized to cleanse the mind, activate the chakras, and promote spiritual development.

Visualization is imagining yourself performing an action in your mind's eye. You see yourself performing the action as if it were true, despite the fact that it is only occurring in your mind. Visualization enables you to become more in tune with your emotions and feelings so that they no longer exert control over you. They serve as a guide for your decisions and actions in life.

To activate the sacral chakra, it is important to incorporate both meditation and visualization into your daily practice. Together, they assist in removing any obstacles that may prevent you from accessing your complete creative potential.

Benefits of Meditation and Visualization in General

Prior to discussing specific techniques for opening the sacral chakra, it is essential to discuss the numerous health advantages meditation and visualization provide. Both practices have been shown to enhance health in numerous ways, such as:

Relaxation

Meditation's first and most apparent benefit is relaxation. Meditation is an effective method for reducing anxiety and tension. When you concentrate on one item, your body can relax and release any tension it may be holding.

Meditation results in better sleep, more vitality, and an overall sense of well-being.

Enhanced Focus

There are simply too many distractions in modern society, according to a prevalent complaint. The media constantly bombards us with information, making it difficult to concentrate on a single topic for an extended period of time. Meditation has been shown to improve concentration and focus, making it simpler to complete tasks without becoming distracted.

Better Sleep

Are you experiencing difficulty sleeping? Studies have shown that meditation improves the quality of your slumber, allowing you to wake up feeling more rested and revitalized. Additionally, it reduces tension and anxiety, two of the most common causes of insomnia. Meditation's calming effect can help you fall asleep faster and remain asleep longer.

Enhanced Immunity

When we experience tension or anxiety, our bodies enter a fight-or-flight state. Our ancestors required this primitive survival mechanism to survive in the outdoors. Unfortunately, this mechanism has not evolved to accommodate modern stresses.

As a result, when we are in a state of chronic stress, our bodies go into overdrive and produce stress hormones that are detrimental to the immune system and wear it down. This results in a variety of health issues, including colds, influenza, and other ailments.

Meditation has been shown to help the body recover from this state of chronic tension, providing a much-needed break for the immune system. Consequently, habitual meditators are less likely to become ill.

Sacral Chakra Unblocking, Healing, and Balancing

Meditation and visualization provide numerous health benefits and can also be used to clear blocked chakras. When this occurs, we draw into our subtle energy body's immense healing potential. This significantly improves mental, emotional, and physical health.

As the sacral chakra is intimately associated with our emotions, many of the benefits we receive when this chakra is activated are related to emotional healing. For instance, we are better equipped to manage challenging emotions such as sadness, anger, and anxiety. We may also realize that we are more receptive to new experiences and creative than we were previously.

You can attempt a variety of methods to open your sacral chakra if you are looking for one. The following section examines some of the most effective meditation and visualization techniques for achieving this objective.

Exercises in Guided Meditation for Opening the Sacral Chakra

Guided meditation is an effective method for achieving inner tranquility and clearing the mind of distractions. One of the most effective methods for opening and balancing the sacral chakra is to engage in guided meditation exercises designed specifically for this energy center. Typically, these exercises involve deep breathing and visualization, allowing you to concentrate on your breath and all associated sensations.

You can use specific visualizations, such as imagining an orange sphere glowing deep within your abdomen, or you can simply concentrate on any sensations that arise, such as vibrations, tingling, or warmth. These guided meditation exercises help you open and strengthen your sacral chakra through regular practice, allowing you to feel more grounded, centered, and in tune with your intuition.

Imagine the Mind to Be a Lake

Imagine your thoughts to be a lake or reservoir. Imagine the water to be clear and tranquil, with gentle ripples. Permit yourself to sink beneath the surface and experience the water's tranquility enveloping you. Imagine the water imparting vitality and renewed energy to your body as you inhale. As you exhale, let go of anything that no longer serves you and observe it dissipate into the water. Continue this visualization for several minutes, or until you experience a sense of inner peace and equilibrium.

Consider the Sacral Chakra to be a Lotus Flower.

Visualize the sacral chakra as a vibrant and alive lotus flower. The lotus develops in murky water, but it emerges as a pure flower. This signifies that even when our lives are filled with obstacles, we can rise above them and reach our full potential. Similarly to how the lotus flower turns to face the sun, we should also face the radiance of our divine nature. We achieve balance and harmony in our lives by visualizing the sacral chakra as a lotus flower.

When you feel prepared, return your attention gradually to the present. Open your eyes slowly and regain normal awareness. To further assimilate the energy of the sacral chakra into your life, you may wish to spend a few moments writing about your experience or engaging in creative visualization exercises.

The Sacral Chakra Clearing Workout

If you prefer a hands-on approach to activating your sacral chakra, this exercise may be suitable for you. This practice entails massaging and applying pressure to the area of the body associated with this energy center in order to clear obstructions and open your energy flow.

Find a comfortable seat to begin. You may cross your legs on the floor or on a chair, but you must position your feet flat on the ground if you choose a chair. Take several long breaths and relax your body. Beginning with both palms, massage your lower abdomen in a clockwise direction. Spend a few minutes massaging in this manner, applying gentle pressure and focusing on any tense or obstructed areas.

Visualize the energies of your sacral chakra expanding and circulating freely. Imagine that you are infusing your body with vitality and healing energy via this chakra. Imagine inhaling the vitality of growth and expansion with every breath. Imagine that, as you exhale, you are releasing tension or negativity from the sacral chakra and witnessing it float away. Continue this visualization for several minutes, or until you sense your sacral chakra opening and energies flowing freely.

Take a few deep breaths and relax your body when you have completed. Spend a few minutes writing about your experience or engaging in creative visualization if you are unsure of the best method to accomplish this. You can learn to open and balance your sacral chakra and experience a greater sense of well-being, creativity, and connection in your life with time and perseverance.

The Psychological Healing Meditation

This guided meditation will assist you if you struggle to comprehend, communicate with, and heal the emotional energy held within your sacral chakra. This practice assists you in recognizing and releasing any negative emotions that are preventing you from achieving balance in this area of your life.

Find a comfortable seat to begin. You have the option of sitting on the floor with your legs crossed or on a chair with your feet horizontal on the ground. Close your eyes and unwind your entire body. Imagine yourself inhaling the radiance of love and healing as you take a few deep breaths. Imagine discharging the tension or negativity from your body as you exhale.

Visualize the energy of your sacral chakra when you are ready. Imagine it as a luminous orb of light in the middle of your lower abdomen. Imagine the light emanating from this chakra to be a magnificent, radiant orange.

Now, concentrate on any emotions residing in the sacral chakra, such as guilt, shame, sorrow, or anger. Simply permit yourself to become aware of these emotions without judging them. Imagine that you are surrounded by the radiance of love and healing as you inhale these emotions.

Permit yourself to completely experience these emotions, and then visualize releasing them. Imagine the emotions evaporating as you exhale and being replaced by the light of love and healing. Continue to take long breaths and focus on releasing the sacral chakra's emotions.

Take a few deep breaths and relax your body when you have completed. Spend a few minutes reflecting on your experience through writing or visualization. You will learn to release the negative emotions that are preventing you from achieving balance in your sacral chakra and achieving greater health, happiness, and fulfillment in your life with time and fortitude.

Mindful Meditation Exercises for Commuting and Walking Outside

Walking is an excellent way to relieve stress and get some exercise, but it's simple to zone out and lose track of the present moment; this is where mindful meditation comes in. Mindful meditation involves being present in the moment and devoting nonjudgmental attention to one's thoughts, feelings, and sensations. It helps you concentrate on the present moment, which can be extremely beneficial when walking outdoors.

One of the simplest methods to practice mindful meditation is to concentrate on your breath. Also, as you walk, give attention to the feeling of your feet striking the ground and your breath entering and leaving your body. It's acceptable for your mind to wander. Bring your focus back to your respiration slowly. You'll experience greater serenity and tranquility in daily life if you meditate more mindfully.

Guidelines for Establishing a Meditation Routine

It is essential to have a consistent time and location for your meditation practice. It facilitates the formation of habits and facilitates consistency. When determining your time and location, be sure to choose a place where you will not be disturbed.

Breathing is one of the most essential components of meditation. Be careful to breathe slowly and deeply. If your mind begins to wander, merely return your focus to your breathing. The objective is not to empty one's consciousness, but rather to concentrate on the present moment.

When meditating, it is essential to maintain a decent posture. This serves to keep your body calm and allows you to concentrate. If you prefer, you can rest in a chair, on the floor with your legs crossed, or even lie down. It is essential that you feel comfortable and at ease.

Do not attempt to meditate for hours on your first try. Start slowly with a few minutes of daily meditation. As you gain experience, gradually increase the length of your meditation sessions. Do not become disheartened if you do not see immediate results. As you persist, the task will become simpler.

If you find it difficult to concentrate or are frequently distracted, record yourself reading your guided meditation. Then, listen to the recording later and use it to help you maintain concentration and focus. Additionally, it is beneficial to have the recorded voice of another person guide you through the meditation.

Use a Timer: If you are new to meditation, it is helpful to use a timer. You need not be concerned with how long you have been meditating. Simply set a timer for the desired duration and concentrate on your respiration until the alarm sounds. Avoid those that have a noisy tick. Over time, you should wean yourself off the timer and instead rely on your internal schedule.

When meditating, it is essential to maintain a focus on your objectives. If you have a specific objective, such as reducing tension or enhancing concentration, keep that objective in mind while you meditate. This maintains your motivation and concentration. To reap the benefits of meditation, it is important to commence slowly, but you must also be consistent. It is beneficial to meditate daily, even if only for a few minutes.

Discover a Community: If you're having trouble maintaining your meditation practice, seek out a community of like-minded individuals. There are numerous groups and seminars available to assist you in learning more about meditation and achieving success in your practice. Joining an online community or finding a regular practice partner are also viable alternatives.

In addition to these guidelines and suggestions, it is essential to be patient with yourself. The more you practice, the greater your improvement will be. Meditation is a process, not an endpoint.

Meditation is an effective method for tapping into your inner resources and achieving your objectives. When used effectively, it helps you improve your focus and concentration, reduce stress, and achieve success. Nonetheless, meditation and visualization are not universal practices. It is essential to experiment and determine what works best for you, as what works for others may not work for you.

There is no right or wrong method to practice meditation or visualization. Discover what works best for you and persist with it. You will be amazed at how much meditation and visualization can help you achieve your objectives with practice and consistency.

Guided Imagery For Clearing Your Solar Plexus Chakra

This visualization will assist you in opening your solar plexus chakra so you can feel more self-assured and empowered in all areas of your life. It will assist you in creating strong connections between your mind and body, which will have a positive effect on all aspects of your existence.

You will begin by taking a few long breaths and, if desired, moving your hands and legs around until you find a comfortable position to hold for the duration of this exercise. Take a moment to gather your thoughts, then close your eyes and settle into your seat. Deeply inhale through your nostril, allowing the vitality of each breath to permeate your entire body. Exhale completely until all air has been expelled from your airways. Gently wiggle both hands one last time to ensure that you are still firmly rooted in the present moment and have complete access to all regions of your body. Three times more, inhale and exhale deeply as you thoroughly settle into your body.

The next stage in this visualization involves imagining a sphere of yellow light one foot in front of you. This orb is your personal source of power, so you must handle it with care and reverence. The orb represents your belief system, and it is what you tell yourself about the future from day to day. It is what maintains your mind focused on positive thoughts so that you can continue living a happy and fulfilling life. Before moving on to the next element of the visualization, consider its size, shape, and general appearance.

Imagine you are now holding one hand upward. As your hand reaches out to touch the sphere, you will sense resistance on your palm. This shove symbolizes all the negative beliefs you have about yourself. If you believe that you cannot change, then that is precisely what will remain fixed in position indefinitely. This visualization is not intended to alter every thought you have ever had. Instead, make some adjustments to get back on track with improving your life in as many ways as possible and restore the solar plexus chakra's proper functioning.

Imagine a much larger sphere of energy encompassing your body, with its center in your solar plexus. This orb of vibrant, radiant yellow light represents your self-assurance and personal strength. Every time a negative thought attempts to attach itself to your energy, this orb will push it away until there is no room for negativity in your psyche. This visualization illustrates how crucial it is to always think positively and fend off negativity before it has a chance to take over.

Feel the room's energy beginning to shift as the negativity that once dominated your existence dissipates into nothingness. Feel your personal power increase as you replace thoughts of despair and dread with positive ones. Observe the hue of the orb in your vicinity intensify and illuminate as your personal power becomes more accessible than ever. Permit your personal orb to completely engulf the one in front of you while your solar plexus shines even brightly than the sun. Feel this primal strength.

Feel the energy of this chakra move like a wave from your solar plexus to your extremities and back again. Permit yourself to become accustomed to how it feels within you and observe how much lighter you feel without the weight of all that negativity. Imagine that when the brilliant energy is in motion, it has joined the cadence of your heartbeat. Notate how much stronger it appears now that these negative beliefs have been eliminated permanently.

You may choose to open your eyes once the orb is glowing intensely and your glowing energy is moving around your body. Upon opening them, you will feel lighter and more confident than before. Hold on to this emotion as a constant reminder to think positively.

Tips and Tricks for Working Effectively with Guided Meditations

It has been demonstrated that using imagery increases the likelihood of success for guided meditation sessions. If you are having difficulty focusing on something, consider visualizing it rather than thinking of it in words. Despite the fact that words are sometimes simpler, try visualizing them through the lens of an image of your choosing. Remember that this image is not required, and you can always just utter the word that represents that concept instead. Visualizing yourself performing a task or observing a scene makes it easier for your mind to focus on the task at hand than it is to listen to someone over sounds that you do not comprehend.

Numerous individuals favor listening to a guided meditation on a continuous repeat. This can be readily accomplished by wearing headphones while practicing. In order to accomplish this, it is helpful to create two separate tracks in an audio editing application such as Audacity. Each recording could be an hour long. Use the first track as background music, and throughout the meditation, add the sound of a mantra. This will make it much simpler for you to concentrate on what is being said during your session, rather than being distracted by background audio or noise. The repetition may also stimulate more positive thoughts than would be possible if you merely read them from a book or some other source. In addition, you can play this audio file as you fall asleep for optimal results.

Initially, some individuals find it simpler to simply listen for five minutes per day than to attempt extended meditations. I would recommend making this a daily routine. You will accomplish much more by meditating for five minutes once or twice daily than by endeavoring to meditate for five days in one day. It is a practice, not a test that you must prepare for and pass with flying colors, only to forget everything you've learned afterward. Therefore, it is in your best interest to determine right now that you will never miss a day of meditation and visualization to help your solar plexus chakra function properly. If you can maintain this behavior for at least 30 days, you will no longer need to remind yourself to do it. You may find yourself doing it while in line at the grocery store or delayed in traffic, or wherever you can find a few minutes to maintain the balance of your solar plexus chakra. You may not even require an audio recording for this.

You will enjoy incorporating "breathwork" into your meditation and visualization practices. The consequences will be catastrophic. What is breathwork and why is it significant? Continue reading to learn more.

Green, the color of rebirth, life, energy, and nature, is a beautiful and invigorating hue associated with growth, safety, the environment, fecundity, and harmony.

Green: The Natural Color

Green is regarded as the most soothing and tranquil color due to the belief that it possesses a potent healing quality. This color occupies a large portion of the color spectrum relative to other colors, which explains why it predominates in the natural environment. This is also why it is frequently used in interior design and decoration. It promotes freshness, tranquility, inner serenity, tranquility, positivity, and strength, all of which are induced by a walk in nature. It has a rejuvenating, calming, and soothing effect on the mind and alleviates anxiety, nervousness, and chronic tension.

Additionally, it is the color associated with banking, finances, and prosperity. Money is frequently represented by the color green, as it is the essence that sustains an economy and our lives, just as green veins transport the nutrients our bodies need to thrive. We use green money to purchase fruit, whereas our progenitors had to cultivate the fruit themselves. The common expression 'turn over a fresh leaf' means to start over. Additionally, green is associated with freshness, development, renewal, and rebirth.

In a negative context, the color can represent envy, ambition, and avarice. Different varieties of the color elicit distinct connotations. Dark green represents wealth, ambition, and greed, olive green represents harmony, and yellow green represents envy, cowardice, and illness.

Green is the color of the fourth chakra.

The heart chakra, also known as 'Anahata' in Sanskrit, which translates to 'unbeaten,' 'unhurt,' or 'unstruck,' is the fourth of the seven chakras and their balance point.

This chakra is located near the heart and is responsible for affection, friendships, relationships, happiness, and compassion. As your heart is associated with compassion and affection, it is the energy center of everything related to your happiness and emotional well-being. It is also associated with tranquility and absolute peace. The heart chakra influences the skin, hands, thymus, heart, chest, lungs, breasts, limbs, and cardiac nerve plexus.

When your heart chakra is balanced, strong green energy travels through it, and you have healthy blood circulation, a strong heart, a strengthened immune system, and you feel physically and mentally fit and healthy. In contrast, an unbalanced heart chakra causes heart issues such as angina and heart attack, neck, arm, and upper body discomfort, lung problems, an overactive or underactive immune system, and muscle tightness.

In addition, an inactive heart chakra causes you to be overly critical, demanding, possess a swollen cranium, and be a perfectionist. In contrast, an overactive heart chakra causes feelings of withdrawal, loneliness, depression, weakness, laziness, and restlessness. In contrast, a balanced heart chakra transforms you into a person who is sociable, intellectual, serene, and poised, with the capacity to comprehend things, form associations, and make logical decisions.

Let us now explore the various meanings of green across cultures and communities.

Diverse Interpretations of the Color Green

The phrase 'green-eyed monster' is indicative of an envious individual. The expression 'green with envy' has a similar connotation.

In the majority of Asian and Eastern cultures, green is associated with eternal and new life, fertility, prosperity, good health, and new beginnings. The color green is also associated with fertility, prosperity, good health, and new beginnings. However, in Chinese culture, males are prohibited from wearing green hats, as this color signifies an infidel wife.

Our next color is blue.

A Third Eye That Is Open

When your third eye is open, you will be able to see things in a positive light and have a much greater ability to see the large picture. It will not matter much what is occurring around you or how bad things appear to be right now. You will understand intuitively that no matter what is happening, everything always works out in the end. A highly developed third eye chakra provides heightened consciousness and spiritual insight. As you are already aware, it is not a component of your corporeal body, but rather your energy body.

A blocked Ajna chakra can result in issues such as difficulty concentrating, difficulty hearing, sore eyes, sinus pain, hallucinations, terrible visual perception, an inability to connect with divine guidance or receive intuitive wisdom, baffling dreams, migraines and headaches, and an inability to see through past illusions. This chapter attempts to provide an answer to the query, "How do you know when your third eye is open?" Let's investigate some of the indicators.

Indicators of an Open Third Eye

You are incredible at discerning deceit. Regardless of the skill of the deceiver or the plausibility of their story, you can always tell when someone is lying. This is both a blessing and a curse, particularly when you're conversing with loved ones and you can tell they're lying.

You have the uncanny ability to instantly shift your entire consciousness to the present moment. As you are aware, the majority of individuals spend their time in the past or the future. They are rarely in the present; even when conversing with you, you can tell they are contemplating what they will say next.

When your third eye is open, you can be firmly rooted in the present. This is not a simple task for people to complete rapidly. On the other hand, you have no difficulty directing your entire attention and concentration to the present moment.

You possess very profound concepts. If you know someone who is a profound thinker, there is a possibility that their Ajna chakra is open. They are exceptionally attuned to the messages their spirit guides convey to them, and their thoughts go far beyond those of the average person. They know better than to assume that things are precisely as they appear, as they are aware that life is full of symbols, with synchronicity and significance surrounding us every day. If this describes you, you are aware that your mind can grasp the nuances and subtleties of ordinary interactions and conversations. In other words, you have the uncanny ability to not only hear what someone actually says, but also what they are not saying. Your third eye is undoubtedly activated if you have a knack for knowing things without understanding their source.

You have utilized your psychic abilities. If you have the ability to perceive information through bodily sensation, you are clairsentient. You are claircognizant if you know things you are not supposed to know and cannot explain how you obtained this knowledge. You are clairaudient if you hear music, voices, or other sounds from the spirit world or from higher entities with messages for you. You are clairvoyant if you can perceive images, visions, or hues that are invisible to others and if you can locate a location, a person, or an event without prior knowledge. You may also encounter telepathy.

You perceive visually. Whenever you are attempting to figure something out or make a decision, you tend to visualize rather than use words.

You are a humble person. When you perform virtuous deeds, you are not seeking recognition. You have no interest in receiving praise. You care little for acknowledgment. You only truly desire to assist others and move on with your existence.

You have acquired the ability to shatter expectations. It is an unfortunate reality that the majority of us make decisions based on the expectations of others. If your third eye is open, you have realized that it does not matter what other people think of your life decisions. You are no longer afraid or motivated to satisfy others. You make decisions based on what is best for you and you alone, and you experience an incredible sense of independence.

You complete the sentences of others. You already know what they're going to say before they've even spoken a word. Typically, you are accurate.

You are an expert at recognizing patterns. You cannot connect the connections where others can because you have a third eye. This also indicates that you are adept at finding unorthodox solutions to problems that require little effort.

Your visions are incredibly descriptive. It is comparable to viewing a 3D movie. Additionally, you can recall every detail of the dream, not just its central motif. Whether it's a good or terrible, realistic or fantastic dream, you can recall every detail. Occasionally, your dreams can be so vivid that you forget you're dreaming, or you could almost argue that you're living a completely different existence than your actual one.

You experience a lot of déjà vu. People, places, and objects you have never knowingly encountered often feel familiar to you for reasons you cannot explain. If this occurs frequently, it indicates that your third eye is open or that you are awakening.

You suffer from increased headaches and migraines. Before concluding that your constant headaches and migraines are the result of your third eye opening, please consult a medical professional to rule out any underlying health conditions. If your doctor declares you to be in perfect health, there is a possibility that you are experiencing discomfort in your head due to the opening of your third eye.

You have heightened sensitivity to sound and light. This is because the third eye enhances depth perception, allowing you to perceive significantly more information than the average individual. Some individuals can also perceive geometric shapes.

You converse with superior beings. People who have their third eye open typically have conversations with spiritual beings and entities from other realms, who frequently have life-improving information to impart. Have you ever had conversations that seem to be occurring in your mind, but whose topics you know nothing about, leaving you to wonder where they are coming from? If you have, there is a high probability that your third eye is open and you are in contact with other beings. If you wish to cultivate a relationship with these entities, all you need to do is state your intention very clearly. Before investigating a relationship with these entities, you must consult a medical professional or therapist if you have a history of mental illness, schizophrenia, or anything similar.

Stories from Individuals with Third Eyes Wide Open

The following are true accounts of individuals who have developed their third vision. To safeguard their privacy, their names have been changed per their request.

Rachel states, "I have always and continue to be an ardent believer in science. However, I never imagined I would be uttering the things I am saying now in the past. I believed chakras and energy bodies were nonsense, so I decided to work skeptically on opening these nonexistent energy centers to prove my point. Prior to ascending to the crown chakra, it was essential to commence with the root chakra. It was insanity when I began working on my third eye chakra!

I was already experiencing some paranormal activity, but then things took a drastic turn for the worse. To make a long tale short, I left a lucrative position as a business consultant to become a Reiki healer because that was my destiny. I realized this was my true vocation when I opened my third eye and gained vision. I have never been more fulfilled or contented in my life."

When Josh opened his third eye, he felt like he had been reborn. I was abruptly overcome by a sensation that I can only describe as 'knowing.' I was able to see through the illusion of duality, discovering that neither right nor wrong exist. Additionally, I was able to see through the illusion of culture and society. It became clear to me that the rules devised for us, including all the shoulds and shouldn'ts, are merely constructs. The universe is a persistent reality, intent on persuading you not to cross certain boundaries. This may sound extremely psychopathic, but it's not as if I'm going to act in a horrible manner to harm others. It's just that gaining this knowledge made me realize that I could readily love my adversaries. Since then, my life has never been the same. The day my third eye was opened,

I was able to discover a connection with even the most unlikely people, and since then, I've received so many wonderful blessings.

When my third eye was open, my mandible was probably literally dangling for hours. Okay, I exaggerated, but the point is that my mind was completely shattered. It felt like a download or stream of consciousness was flooding into me, and all of a sudden I had a profound understanding of life on a level I had never, ever, ever before encountered. It was transformative.

Nuru says, "While I was in the midst of a third-eye meditation, I abruptly found myself viewing an entirely different scene from a microscopic perspective. I am truly at a loss for words to convey this. When I emerged from this, I realized that something extraordinarily significant had just occurred. During the next two hours, I had the impression that I was receiving very profound and divine information about existence, the universe, myself, and what I needed to do on Earth. I didn't just comprehend spirit. I was aware."

Siobhan states, "When I first opened my third eye, I was confident in my abilities and well-prepared. In retrospect, I recognize I was anything but. I witnessed atrocities that, to this day, I cannot adequately describe. It felt like I existed and did not exist simultaneously. The more I attempted to make sense of my experience, the less sense it made. After that, I felt like I had lost my identity for many months, and nothing in life brought me pleasure. I was forced to shut my third sight. When I am ready, if I am ever again ready, I will attempt again.

"Because I opened my third eye, I was able to experience things I never thought possible," says Lawrence. I had numerous out-of-body experiences, lucid dreams, and conversations with God and other superior beings. I was also able to connect with my spirit guide, with whom I've been collaborating to accomplish my life's purpose. Also, the synchronicities I encounter on a daily basis are insane."

Kosi states, "There was a time when my residence was filled with unexplainable negative energy. Even my family, who at the time had little interest in spirituality, could sense something was amiss. In one of my visions, I practiced Transcendental Meditation and worked on my third eye chakra. In that dream, I was in an exact replica of my house, though it was significantly darker. I immediately queried the man who was sitting on my sofa, "Am I dreaming?" I've never forgotten anything he said to me. "Wherever you find yourself awake, it is not a dream." He then transformed into a terrifying creature that pursued me throughout my house. Just as it was about to grab me in a corner, I was abruptly overcome with righteous rage and courage, and I ripped the thing apart with my hands. As soon as I did so, its body vanished into thin air. When I awoke the next morning, I realized this was no ordinary dream, and my family began to comment on how much lighter the house felt."

Is My Third Eye Activated?

This brief quiz will determine whether or not your third eye is open or awakening.
Do you experience vivid dreams?
Have you ever experienced pulsating or fluttering in the center of your third eye?
Do you feel, when you close your eyes, that there is an interior light in your head?
Are you exceptionally light-sensitive?
Do you frequently experience headaches?
Have you observed that certain numbers appear frequently, whether in the time, a phone number, a billboard, or elsewhere?
Have you ever yearned for a greener, healthier diet for no apparent reason?
Consider you to be one with all of existence and that no one is distinct?
Do you perceive auras around others?

Do you frequently contemplate the meaning of life?

Do you ever feel like you're living in a literal matrix while everyone else seems to be sleeping?

Have you ever had profound ideas that popped into your mind for no apparent reason?

Do you find yourself guided by something that seems intelligent outside of your typical working life?

Is déjà vu a regular occurrence for you?

Have you noticed a transition in your musical preferences toward more positive and uplifting material?

Sometimes do you hear a low or high pitch that seems to originate in your head?

If you answered yes to the majority of these queries, it is possible that your third eye is fully functional. If your response was negative, do not be disheartened. All you need to do is take your time with the procedure, as it will not be completed in a single day. This book contains the accounts of individuals who have devoted their time and energy to awakening the third eye chakra. If you feel like you've put in the time and effort, but nothing is happening, you must verify that your intention to open your third eye is sincere and unambiguous. If it is, then there is no need for concern. Eventually, it will transpire. The last thing you want to do is fret or obsess over the fact that it is not yet open, as this will only set you back and attract negative energies and thoughts that you could do without.

Discover Your Love With The Heart Chakra

The Heart Chakra

The fourth chakra is the center of the seven chakras, with three chakras below and three chakras above. This is where the physical and the spiritual converge. The fourth chakra, also known as the heart chakra, is located in the center of the chest and consists of the heart, cardiovascular plexus, thymus organ, lungs, and breasts. Additionally, it regulates the lymphatic system. The Sanskrit term for the fourth chakra is Anahata, which translates to "unhurt." The name suggests that beneath the wounds and grudges of past interactions resides a profound place where there is no pain.

When your heart chakra is open, you are overflowing with compassion; you are quick to forgive and acknowledge others and yourself. The anahata chakra is associated with affection, compassion, and contentment. It is the source of profound and significant principles that cannot be expressed through language. Anahata is a link between the lower and upper chakras that connects the physical world to the spiritual realm. Air is also the element of the heart chakra. Like the element of the heart chakra, air, affection is all around and within each individual.

Some people reside in the location of grievances. They have been harmed by their parents, acquaintances, or lovers in the past. Everyone has encountered these issues at some point. It is difficult to avoid situations in which someone might endeavor to harm you. However, you have the option to choose how to proceed in this circumstance. Some individuals may attempt to harm the offender in return. However, that is not living from an Anahata position. The person who inflicts suffering on others is motivated by fear, a lack of awareness, or contempt, all of which indicate a closed heart chakra.

When you experience wounded feelings from the past or the present, you can either let them go or cling to them. By releasing them, you are able to open your heart to new people and new experiences with compassion, love, and understanding. Clinging to these feelings or allowing negative emotions to grow will eventually cut you off from opportunities to love and serve. Making a decision is all that is required to release these feelings. This activity will provide mental tranquility.

Consequently, this chakra is accountable for visualizing the life stream through the beating of the heart focus, and it regulates the flow of blood. The heart supports the structure of all body cells. Additionally, it energizes the largest nerve of the parasympathetic sensory system. When it is opened, it enables us to expel foreboding fragments and cultivates the type of profound affection. Through our Heart Chakra, we can experience a sense of connection and oneness with others.

Advantages of a Healthy Heart Chakra

When the heart chakra is in harmony, you will experience feelings of affection, joy, compassion, and euphoria. Additionally, this activity will bring you closer to the people around you.

Discord in the Heart Chakra:

Here are the mental manifestations of a blocked heart chakra:

Co-dependence

Manipulative conduct

a sense of unworthiness

Degrading self-esteem

Lack of self-assurance

In addition, the physical manifestations of a blocked heart chakra are as follows:

cardiac disorders

Lungs difficulties

Chest discomfort

poor circulation of blood

Variability in blood pressure

Love Using the Heart Chakra

To begin, put yourself in the shoes of another person. Although this is difficult to accomplish, it can be beneficial for fostering empathy. Imagine situations in which the impolite person may have found themselves in order to develop sympathy and empathy. When encountering a man who is being disagreeable or who has treated you poorly in the past, quickly run through a large number of what-if scenarios. As you create these scenarios, whose possible outcomes are incalculable, you begin to empathize with the other person and his or her situation. This strategy removes you from your own self-indulgence and places your compassion on the other person. Moreover, if you have a relative or a close friend who repeatedly displays harmful behavior towards you, you can express affection and compassion for that person. However, you must establish boundaries and limitations for this action. Additionally, realize that when someone harms you, it is never about you, but about them.

Give Love to Receive Love

The best way to obtain affection is to grant it. Leo Buscaglia, a motivational lecturer, used to argue that we should give and receive 12 hugs per day for optimal health. Therefore, give much affection.

Additionally, there are numerous methods to express affection. Among them are the following:

Smile at daily acquaintances. Despite the possibility that you don't want to, you should always smile when you meet someone. Start using this method, and the outcomes will be overwhelming.

Forgive others and avoid holding grudges.

Give your companions, family, and coworkers positive affirmations and constructive criticism.

Try to spend one day per week without criticizing anyone or anything, including yourself.

Utilize any available opportunity to cultivate affection and adoring emotions. Whatever you give will be returned to you by love.

Methods for Opening the Heart Chakra

The heart chakra is one of the body's most important focal points. This chakra allows you to fill your existence with love and happiness. Some of the methods that love can help you to open your heart chakra are as follows:

Be honest with your emotions

Whether you record them or exclaim for everyone to hear, you must allow them an opportunity to escape. Declare what is in your spirit. It is generally excruciating, but it is part of the healing process. Even if you have no intention of anyone else reading what you communicate, it is incredibly helpful to articulate your emotions in order to become more accepting, mindful, and content.

Avoid being attached

It is commonly believed that you will receive what you give to others. However, yoga practice genuinely aids in achieving self-satisfaction and contentment. Continuing to dwell on past events and problems is detrimental. Additionally, it ensures that we either fear the future or dwell in the past. As with most things in life, it is easier to say than to do. Assist yourself and systematically chisel away at this.

Understand how to accept things as they are.

As a rule of thumb, it is preferable to disregard something that cannot be altered. There is no need to fret or worry about something over which you have no control. When you have no control over a situation, it is best to let them go and cease intimidating you. It is both a futile and vital exercise. Instead, focus on what you can influence. This is the item that will bring you happiness and satisfaction. Set daily objectives and follow the path of least resistance.

After learning to let go of the negative aspects of your life, you realize that love is the most powerful healer in the world. Ultimately, the ability of loving oneself is the happiness that everyone seeks. Keeping this expectation in mind during asana practice will expand your consciousness. Some of the most effective postures for cardiac opening are as follows:

Camel posture

Falcon posture
Back rotating drills.

Moreover, the color green regulates the heart chakra. Therefore, consume a lot of dull green verdant vegetables and take green beverages. Additionally, Bija Mantras are an excellent method for opening the chakra. Use these techniques to let go of all negative emotions and to fill your heart with love and compassion for everyone.

About Reflection

Synopsis

A substantial number of practices are required for extraterrestrial existence; some are physical, while others are fundamental. There are rhyming exercises, such as chanting religious psalms or physically sitting on the wheel of prayer to God.

Now that it's out in the open, some individuals perform specific physiological body sshedules prior to attempting extraordinary feats. Nonetheless, reflection is one of the primary exercises that connects both profound and physical exercises.

This is the method by which a great number of extraterrestrials tend to associate with their inner profound domain and even join with God. Taking everything into account, not everyone understands the significance of reflection in profound sense of being. This must be clarified by appreciating the power of reflection.

Vehind It

Reflection is a crucial tool for anyone who wishes to grow profoundly. Unease tends to affect those who disregard contemplation. Note the distinction between ds-directness and illness. The most recent is a bodily isue, whereas the other is an otherworldly isue that results in dstress.

This is fundamentally accomplished through this disengagement with God. In relation to this, contemplation tends to unite our souls with God, thereby fostering the growth of the fundamental self. This is the primary reflection force regarding the unearthly.

Essentially, it is believed that reflection has benefits for the mind, body, and spirit. This is due to the fact that the three are interconnected to form the real you. Regarding the Scripture, its support is derived from our association with God, which is attained through regular reflection. Therefore, not ruminating deprives the sririt of nourishment.

This is perilous, comparable to depriving the body of nourishment. We may end up starving to death if we follow this pattern, as will the sririt. A body without a sririt is also considered 'deceased'. If you are experiencing uneasiness, it is a sign that your soul is hungry. Make a move before tings deteriorate.

Additionally, there are various levels of contemplation, each designed to meet a particular need. Numerous individuals have the desire to ponder but end up perplexed due to a lack of results. Why do you believe this occurs? It is primarily due to the fact that they perform the incorrect contemplation exercises for their level, thereby producing no results.

For more information on contemplation levels, consult a contemplation master, who will provide guidance on the various contemplation levels and their applications. Along these corridors, you will be able to pick.

The Third Chakra, The Sacral Chakra

The Naval chakra is located just behind the navel and controls the body's vital digestive organs, including the stomach, digestive system, large intestine, adrenal glands, liver, and pancreas. It is advisable, when visualizing the location of the navel chakra, to press your fingertips approximately two inches above the navel, on your stomach and back.

Diversity and presentation

This chakra's color is yellow, the color of the sun, and its element is fire, representing the energy it can transform to give you the determination to pursue your objectives. Also associated with this chakra is the ram.

Description

If the sacral chakra is concerned with understanding one's desires, the naval chakra is concerned with knowing how to assert them in life. This is where your aspirations can become a reality through planning and implementation. With a healthy navel chakra, your objectives and actions should not be affected by the opinions of others, regardless of how negative they may be. Manipura, which in Sanskrit means "the city of jewels," is frequently depicted as a lotus flower with ten leaves and a downward-pointing red triangle in the centre. According to some sources, the ten leaves represent mental states such as spiritual ignorance, thirst, jealousy, treachery, shame, fear, disgust, delusion, foolishness, and sorrow that emanate from this chakra. A person with a balanced naval chakra will be able to assert themselves in groups, feel in control, have adequate self-esteem, and readily express their will. In addition, they would have the desire to pursue their aims and aspirations, be aware of their intellectual capacities, and be cognizant of their personal responsibility. Physically, they would have a strong core and be able to walk with confidence, drawing strength from a strong core and legs (remember that a healthy naval chakra is only feasible if the root and sacral chakras are also healthy). Because the navel chakra is associated with physical symptoms such as poor digestion, ulcers, pancreas, liver or kidney problems, intestinal tumours, colon disease, and weight issues with an emotional root, such as anorexia and bulimia, they would also have a healthy metabolism and healthy digestion.

What occurs when this chakra is deficient?

When the chakra is underactive, you may lack self-confidence and, as a result, find it difficult to achieve their goals in group settings, allowing others to have their way. You may be indecisive and passive, believing that the opinions of others are superior to your own. You may experience feelings of inadequacy or find yourself perpetually in the midst of an argument or everyone else's desires, with the impression that your own needs are corroding. If your navel chakra is underactive, you may also find it difficult to trust the people around you and your own feelings and emotions, or you may attempt to avoid them entirely by engaging in compulsive behaviors or addictions. You may be someone who continually seeks the approval of others and lacks complete confidence in his own abilities. This can cause you to become quite dependent on having certain people in your life; you may appreciate their company more out of a need for their approval than out of a desire to spend time with them.

What occurs if this chakra becomes overactive?

When the navel chakra is overactive, you can be extremely dominant and even aggressive when interacting with individuals and groups. You may be a perfectionist, always seeking to improve something rather than admitting that it is already satisfactory. You may be judgmental and critical of those around you as well as yourself, but you may not confess it to anyone. You may also have a great deal of rage and be quite determined to always get your way.

Perfectionism and intransigence can turn you into a workaholic or someone who spends too much time planning rather than doing. If the navel chakra is overactive, you may find yourself exploiting your power or manipulating others.

How do you regulate and clear your navel chakra?

The navel chakra is associated with the digestive organs, so examining your diet is a smart place to start. You can find more information on what foods to eat later in this chapter, but in general, it is about balancing your food intake to provide your body with everything it needs, such as having a healthy balance of protein, vegetables, and carbohydrates. Since the navel chakra is associated with self-assurance, self-acceptance, and the realization of one's aspirations, daily affirmations can also assist in unblocking the navel chakra. You can write positive affirmations about yourself on a piece of paper and read them aloud every morning, allowing the energy they convey to embrace you. Try one of these if you are at a loss: "I love and accept myself." I am deserving of others' affection, respect, and kindness. I am proud of my accomplishments and I live an honest existence. I am at ease with myself and my neighbors.

If you have a demanding schedule, try meditating for just a few minutes every night before bed and writing down three things you are grateful for. During the course of a day, many things can occur, but we tend to focus on the negatives while disregarding the positives, thereby creating an inaccurate impression of ourselves. This exercise will help you view your day in a positive light, and if you continue it for at least a month, it should rewire your brain to automatically pursue the positive. If you recognize yourself as a perfectionist or a person with excessive stubbornness, attempt to let go of any rigid beliefs or inflexible methods. Use your obstinacy to fuel your dreams and objectives, bringing them to fruition. If you find yourself to be quite dominant in groups, attempt to soften your approach by listening attentively and empathizing with others. The navel chakra can be unblocked by core-strengthening activities, such as pilates or swimming.

Asanas to activate the navel chakra in yoga:

Again, the greatest poses for the navel chakra are those that strengthen your core, purify your internal organs, and make you feel more powerful. You can regularly practice 'power yoga' to clear your navel chakra, as it consists of yoga poses that improve your strength, balance, and flexibility. For this chakra, it is essential that you focus on your respiration.

Shining Skull Breath. This exercise can help you discharge toxins from your body and revitalize your mind, resulting in a 'shining forehead' with a keen intellect. Focus on the lower abdomen as you sit comfortably with your legs crossed, exhaling in a rapid burst and then allowing the abdomen to re-charge as the air fills your lungs again. To locate the navel chakra, you can cup your hands and gingerly press them into your stomach if you have difficulty with this exercise. Then, press them into your stomach as you exhale a large amount of air. Release your palms and allow your stomach to refuel. You can begin slowly, repeating ten times and breathing in and out roughly every two seconds – whichever is most pleasant for you. Eventually, you can increase the pace and intensity. Aim for 30 cycles initially, then progressively increase this number to at least 100.

The Lion stance. This is an excellent pose for boosting immunity and relieving anger and tension. You can move into the Lion Pose from a seated position. Your legs should be bent and placed behind you so that your pelvis are resting on your heels. Spread your legs as far apart as is suitable for you. Inhale to extend your spine towards the crown of your cranium as you inhale. Exhale and place your palms on the floor in front of your knees with your fingertips pointing towards your heels. Still on the same exhale, arch your spine while gazing up at the point between your eyes, stick out your tongue, and roar like a lion if you desire!

Meditation

Try visualizing the navel chakra point just above your navel as you sit still and meditate, and position your hands on your stomach. Try the hand pose for this chakra by joining the tips of your fingertips, which should be pointing away from you, to form a triangle. Cross your thumbs and extend your fingers. Additionally, you can chant the sound 'RAM'. You may release the sound 'RAM' as you exhale, if desired, by inhaling deeply into your stomach and then exhaling again. Visualize yourself stepping into and being enveloped by a luminous yellow light; if possible, perform this meditation outdoors, surrounded by pools of sunlight. Imagine the radiance of this light purifying your body's organs and granting you the courage to pursue your ambitions.

Diet & Nutrition

Yellow-colored foods are optimal for this chakra, as you may have already surmised. In addition to balancing your diet, if you are currently consuming too much sugar, starch, or fat, try incorporating these yellow-colored foods into your diet: replace your cereal with granola containing bee pollen and a dash of organic honey. Toast some whole wheat bread as a substitute. Eat a banana as a snack and incorporate some maize into your salads. Before going to bed, attempt to calm your mind by drinking peppermint or calming chamomile tea and inhaling the aromas deeply, allowing yourself to experience it with all of your senses.

The Significance of the Seven Chakras in Chapter 4

Beginning with the crown chakra, this chapter describes the characteristics, attributes, and inherent qualities of each chakra.

Throat Chakra

This chakra represents the highest level of energy and is located at the crown of the cranium. It is called Sahasrara in Sanskrit, and it is violet in color. This chakra is represented by a lotus flower with thousands of petals. This chakra has spiritual significance because it represents Shiva or consciousness. Since it is at the apex, it represents the unification of all colors and can be considered the body's prism. This chakra represents intelligence and Divine compassion in the form of wisdom. It is associated with the pineal gland in the body and provides this organ with the necessary energy to function effectively. It is typically characterized as the portion of the brain above the right eye. This chakra is associated with the pearl, which symbolizes purity and quality. This chakra is associated with the movement of the planet Pluto, and those who possess it are known as egomaniacs or leaders. This chakra indicates that the possessor is knowledgeable and enlightened in a variety of areas. Most significantly, this chakra is recognized as the location of the spirit's connection point. The Crown chakra is responsible for integrating the activities of all the other chakras. It is paired with level one, or the root chakra, with which it governs the lower chakras. It is said that controlling the lower level chakras aids in attaining a spiritual level.

Third Eye Chakra

This is the Ajna chakra, also known as the sixth chakra. This chakra is located near the eyebrows or between the eyes on the forehead. It is represented by the color indigo, and its origin is a seed or Aum. This chakra is represented by a triangle that descends within a circle. This chakra represents illumination or intuition. Reaching this chakra requires the ability to govern oneself. Along with enhancing the capacity for imagination, it fosters intuition and wisdom. It affects the pituitary gland, as well as the brain, eyes, ears, sinuses, and spinal cord, among others. Its associated gemstone is diamond, and its planet is the sun. This demonstrates the strength of this chakra, as the sun represents illumination. It is also known for awakening the sixth sense and affecting the higher states of consciousness. This chakra is linked to the sacral chakra, which is located on the second level. This chakra's overuse or activity heightens the analytical and intellectual faculties. If this chakra is underactive, confusion and lack of mental clarity result. This chakra is also known for instilling within a person the qualities of forgiveness and compassion. It makes a person more empathetic towards others and helps to awaken the spirit within them. This is why it is called the third eye chakra, because the third eye is the eye of the soul, the eye of the immortal.

Tongue Chakra

This is the fifth level chakra, known in Sanskrit as Vishuddha. This is located in the throat region of a person and is represented by a pale blue color. This chakra's seed is Hum, and its symbol is a minor modification of the symbol for the sixth chakra; it consists of a circle within a descending triangle. The location of this chakra indicates its function, which is to improve discourse and communication. It fosters creativity, encourages intuitive thought, and instills the desire to communicate and interact with others. It promotes self-expression and compels one to speak the truth. It also regulates the thyroid gland, lungs, gastrointestinal tract, and both arms. It is associated with the gemstone sapphire, and its motion is related to Saturn. This chakra is associated with the sense of hearing, and its combination with level three is known as the solar chakra. Excessive activity of this chakra leads to judgmental thoughts about others and can sometimes result in harmful speech. Less activity of this chakra results in ineffective emotional expression and diminished self-esteem. This chakra is essentially the body's communication core. It is responsible for a person's creativity and helps them realize the importance of telling the truth. Sometimes, we feel as if someone inside of us urges us to speak the truth. This chakra produces the sound of that voice. Consequently, this chakra facilitates the maintenance of relationships with others and connects the world to the psyche.

Throat Chakra

The fourth chakra is the heart chakra, known in Sanskrit as the Anahata. This chakra is located in the center of the human thorax, and its color is pink or green. This chakra contains a Yum seed, and its symbol consists of two intertwined triangles, one ascending and the other declining. This chakra represents air and engenders feelings of compassion and affection. A person who can activate this chakra is known to have an open heart, balanced emotions, and the ability to bring harmony to others. This chakra is associated with the heart, lungs, liver, and thymus, and it promotes healthy blood flow. Its gemstone component is ruby, and its planetary component is Venus. This chakra enhances the perception of touch and has no counterpart among the other chakras. It is coupled to itself. Excessive activation of this chakra results in an inappropriate emotional expression and can also result in inadequate emotional expression. If this chakra's energy is deficient, the individual exhibits ruthless behavior and is emotionless. Consequently, this chakra is the center of affection and emotions. It is also the central chakra among the seven, and is therefore regarded as a link between the higher and lower chakras.

Solar Plexus Chakra

In Sanskrit, this chakra is known as Manipura and is referred to as the "illustrious gem." It is yellow in color, and its seed is known as Ram. This chakra is represented by a triangle with a downward or descending shape. This chakra is associated with fire because it has solar characteristics. It provides feelings of power and pleasure, as well as self-respect. It allows the individual to feel motivated and in control of his will. It also improves relationships with others. This chakra is associated with the pancreas, the liver, the bladder, and the stomach. It is represented by the emerald gemstone, and its planet is

Jupiter. It is associated with the fifth chakra, and its overabundance leads to egocentric beliefs. Its deficiency results in diminished self-esteem. It is located in the center of the body, where the majority of energy is concentrated.

Sacral center

This chakra is associated with the color orange, the planet Mercury, and the Vam seed. It is known as Swadhistana in Sanskrit, and its symbol is a crescent pointing upwards. Its composition is water, and it enhances relationships, sexuality, and feelings of empathy. Its gemstone is amethyst, and it regulates the taste bud. It is associated with the legs and reproductive organs, and its excess causes a sense of addiction. A lack of this chakra causes an emotional closure.

Root Chakra

This chakra is called Muladhara and is located at the base of the spine. It is represented by the color red, the planet Mars, and the gemstone coral. It is represented by a square and composed of earth. It is known to inspire emotions of security and confidence. It regulates the kidneys, spine, urinary bladder, and sense of scent. If it is excessive, it produces feelings of possessiveness, and if it is insufficient, it results in a lack of stability.

www.ingramcontent.com/pod-product-compliance
Lightning Source LLC
Chambersburg PA
CBHW050246120526
44590CB00016B/2239